Brand New Day

poems by
Dave Morrison

2007 JukeBooks
copyright© 2007 by Dave Morrison

All rights reserved under International and Pan American Copyright Conventions. Published in the United States by JukeBooks and lulu Press.

Grateful acknowledgements are due to the editors of the following publications where some of these poems first appeared:

Laura Hird
Cerebral Catalyst
34th Parallel
Courier Publications
Hot Metal Press
thieves jargon
Main Channel Voices

Library of
Congress Cataloging-in-Publication Data

Morrison, Dave

Brand New Day / Dave Morrison

ISBN   978-0-6151-5163-2

For more information about Dave Morrison please visit
www.dave--morrison.com

Book Design by Luther MacNeal

For Susan.

And Anna & Albert.

And Keith Moon, who, asked to rate himself as a drummer said that he was "the best Keith-Moon-style drummer in the world."

And Lawrence Ferlinghetti, who was at one time the most-read living American poet, and has never held a job at a university, never received government funding, and never attended an MLA conference, never won a Pulitzer. And got out of Yonkers.

The less effort, the faster and more powerful you will be.

Bruce Lee

Contents

A Norton Commando, Say	9
Announcement	10
Applause	11
Black & white	12
blues	13
Book	14
Calling Out Around the World	16
Care to join?	17
Carnival	18
Change	19
Consider Yourself	20
Cowboy Song	21
Creation	22
Dad's Favorite Joke	23
Day 1	25
Divine Wind	28
Dog as Poet	29
Drums Along the Interstate	30
Everything	32
Fear®	33

Folk Song Hero	35
Four Days in November	37
Genius	38
Get Ready	39
Glass	41
Goliath	43
Gratitude II	45
Healthy Outlook	46
How to Tend a Fire	47
I Am a Product of a Transistor Radio	48
I Couldn't Sleep	50
I'll Give You Something to Cry About	54
Jazz	55
JC w/ ADD	56
Jerry Lee	58
Joy Wins	59
Letter to Khrushchev	60
like a whip	61
Love	62
Lover Overheard	63

Lucinda Williams, How Could You?	64
My Love	65
New Motto	66
New Voice	67
Not Going Back	68
of course	69
Old Man	71
Our Original Purpose	72
Picking a fight With a New Yorker	74
Poems for Restless Children #7	75
poem notes	76
Remembering Carl	77
Rough Tuesday	78
Something Must Be Done	80
String Theory	82
Texas	83
Thank God for Friends	84
That's the One	85
the Kiss	86
Woodshed	87
Workbench	88

A Norton Commando, say

There's nothing
quite like it.
For one thing, the
smell never quite goes away,
like the musk of illicit
lunch-hour sex, that perfume of
gas, oil, rubber, leather.

The give of the springs, the
saddle that roughly cups your ass,
pedals and grips and pegs that
arrange you like a
supple glove on a
bony hand.

Stand, and bounce on the
starter like a diver on a board,
resuscitate the inert
cast-iron heart, awaken it
coughing and roaring and
hungrily breathing in.

The vibration travels like
a thought – spine to guts to
shoulders to hands and
back again. You've
given life to this
dutiful monster, and now you're going to
hump it down the street, who
cares who hears? You're
riding a wild boar, you've got
a rocket under your balls, your
notion of movement is different from
other peoples.

Oh, man
there's nothing like a
motorcycle.

Maybe one day I'll ride one.

Announcement

The Universe has decided that,
for the moment, you are not going to
get what you want. It may have nothing to do with
how deserving you may or may not be;
on the other hand, maybe it does.
In that joke-y way the Universe has, sometimes it is
in direct inverse proportion to
how badly you want it.

Don't think that the Universe gives a shit about
that sour-grapes-fuck-this-I-hate-writing show
you just put on, either. Nor does the Universe really care
about
the shrinking amount of
time you have. Wallace Stevens had a
numbing job too, and he still found time
to get famous and
duke it out with Hemmingway.

Go ahead, get loaded, what
good will that do? Smash something?
Please. The best you can do is
wait it out, and when the
Universe has forgotten about tonight,
kick it in the ass at
the top
of the
stairs.

Applause

Speed thrilled him and
speed killed him. So
noise and smoke were his
tribute.

In front of the building
orange cones around a silver
hearse, a parade of pickups doing
wheel stands.

The people, mostly young,
butt in lip, baby on hip gave
each smoking truck a
standing O.

22 years old.

Home, I turned on the
radio. A young woman
debuts with the Boston Symphony
Orchestra over her college break.

Graceful and nimble-fingered, she
plays difficult passages with
great speed, and gets a
standing O.

22 years old.

I am 47 and
still alive. In the
kitchen I clap
for myself.

Black & white

Be thankful for strong feelings,
even if they are painful.

Be thankful
for odd dreams, even if you wake up
confused.

Be thankful for Technicolor
fear, regret in deep, rich hues, solid gold
heartache, fireworks of confusion, the
Panavision of despair.

What do you want?

Black and white?

blues

The blues sits on my steps
waiting to walk me to work,
blues the sharp cop, I

the clumsy thief who always
gets caught.
the blues is old and wise and

laughs at the jealous notion that
only certain kinds of people
get the true visitation.

The blues is like Death with a short
attention span – he'll
get you when he wants, but just as likely

turn you loose.

Book

Once
I wrote a book.
A whole book, hundreds
of pages, with words on all of them, words
crawling like ants across a counter, words
all carefully chosen to
change the expression on the reader's
face. The words were nailed together
into paragraphs, like a carpenter frames a
new house, a brand new house, and the paragraphs were
built in neighborhoods of chapters, and the
chapters were like states in a great nation of story, and
it was awesome and unbelievable that I, lousy
student and day-jobber, had gone from ants to a
Great Nation of Story, with only
a computer and coffee and time.
I asked my friend the writer to
write me a recommendation, so I could
get into college, even though I was not young.
"He has written a book" he wrote,
"not a very good book, but a book nevertheless, and that is something."

He was right. It wasn't a very good book.
You know what? I know a man who
built his own house, and OK it's not a very good
house, but how many people can
build their own house? Can you?
My friend the writer never built his own
fucking house. Most people don't, you know why?
Because it's very very hard to do.

So.
I wrote another book.
I guess it was better, I can't really tell.
Then another.
I finally wrote one that was pretty good and you know what?
I'm exhausted. I don't know if I like writing books. I've
built an empty neighborhood where no one but me will live.
But you know what? I know another man who builds

birdhouses – nothing fancy, just nice odd little birdhouses, and the birds like them and so does he. He gives them away, and that's fine.

Calling Out Around the World

plastic transistor, red & white
with a kickstand made of bent chrome wire
AM stations late at night
Gimme shelter, Light my fire
DJs lit my ragged dreams
with a kind of dim and holy light
that boiled my longing into steam
through a plastic transistor, red & white

A keyhole to a bigger world
a needle of light in my dark room
risk and motion, heat and girls
a carnival, a sonic boom
the power of a single song
a thunderclap, a tilt-a-whirl
I squinted through it all night long
that keyhole to a bigger world

people fought, people raced
people yearned and searched and kissed
people left familiar place
then sang about the place they missed
people danced out in the street
dreams created, dreams erased
love and loss – bittersweet,
people fought, and people raced

Plastic transistor, red & white
beams that blast through walls and doors
guitars and drums and dynamite
a place I'd never seen before
DJs lit my ragged dreams
with a kind of dim and holy light
that boiled my longing into steam
through a plastic transistor, red & white

Care to Join?

No,
thank you. Because if I
do, we might become a group,
and we might start to think
like a group, and if
more people join, we could become a large group,
and sometimes large groups
make you pay dues, and the
problem with that is
that the group could become
wealthy, and wealth becomes
power, and in my opinion, every group that
becomes large and wealthy and powerful sooner
or later starts to rot from the
inside out, starts to lose their
humanity, starts to get paranoid
and brutal, starts to lose their ability to
recognize bad choices and
repulsive behavior, and starts to think
that they are better than anyone else, and that
maybe some of the people in the group aren't
good enough to be in the group, and start to think that
anyone not in the group isn't worth a
damn, and they become this huge slobbering
thing that just eats and shits and eats and shits
and eats, and sooner or later this group becomes like
a drunken sumo wrestler, so that it either topples itself,
or is brought down by a smaller leaner more determined
foe,
who then begins to eat and shit and eat and shit, and we
never learn anything
and it just goes on forever and makes you lose faith in
the human race, so no,
thanks,
I'd just as soon not
join.

Carnival

In Brazil it is Carnival,
and the images of bronze
bare-breasted women in
outrageous plumage and paint are
obscene, only because here in
Maine everything is frozen
solid, and we can
only assume that we have
interesting shapes
under these layers.

Outside the squirrel, tail plumage
held high, shakes his ass and
sambas down the
rail fence.

Change

A murder of crows
descended, displacing
an exaltation of larks.

Consider Yourself

If music breaks your
heart, consider yourself
lucky.

Better to know which long
needle is piecing you,

better to know the source of the
excruciating sweetness.

Better that it feel more like a
gift than a wound,

better to feel yourself disassembled and
transformed into an
undulating vibration.

If music breaks your heart, at least
you've had a home, even if you can't
find your way back.

If music breaks your heart,
consider yourself
holy.

Cowboy Song
for Jett

I dreamed I was a cowboy, and
my hands were rough and strong
I squinted against a hot wind, and
my hair was tangled and long

I dreamed I was a cowboy, and
my body no longer felt pain, and
my soul went in every direction, like
the wind over the plain.

I dreamed I was a cowboy
beaten by the sun's cruel rays
my belly was hard and flat, I
hadn't eaten for two days

I dreamed I was a cowboy, and
my body no longer felt pain, and
my soul went in every direction like
the wind over the plain.

I woke up, in a room, in a city
outside I felt the traffic throb
I had to get moving and get on a train or
I'd be late for my job

I squinted against a cold wind as
I pushed my way onto the train, and
my soul went in every direction like
the wind over the plain.

Creation

It was a dark
and stormy night. The
refrigerator shuddered and was
still.

She sat at the
kitchen table and wrote
a poem. In it she placed a
man with a limp, a woman with

a baby, a wedding celebration in
a tavern, a mill closing, a dog carrying
a found wallet in his teeth, a lost child
being comforted by a drunken priest, two

young lovers having sex in a cemetery.
The paper glowed with the life she had
written on it, like phosphorus, like swamp
gas or fireflies, and she gathered and

shaped this light as if gently packing a
snowball and then hurled it into orbit
through the open window.

Dad's Favorite Joke

As she walked up
the path to the State Hospital she
saw him –
he was kneeling in a flowerbed
working with grace and purpose
humming to himself.
Over his shoulder, squinting,
he smiled and said hello. She
took in the bouquets of
color that hugged the hard
walls.
How beautiful! she cried, forgetting
the mask of professionalism
she had applied in the parking lot,
Did you do all this?
He blushed. Oh, it's just
a hobby. She looked at his
clothes, and remembered where
they were, and blurted Are you?
That is, do you?
He laughed. A patient? Oh, not
really. I come here sometimes to get
quiet, get my balance. The world can be
a hectic place.
She agreed, and looked at the growing things,
the quiet order of the beds.
I can't make things grow, she sighed…what I'd give for
a garden like this.
I have a little business on the
side, he said. I do a little landscaping on the
weekends…
She nodded, picturing the rented cottage with
its stubbled lawn and barren beds. The place
needed life.
I'd like that, she said. He wrote a number
on a piece of paper and she promised to
call him on Friday. Smoothing her dress
she carried the brand-new briefcase
through the heavy doors to her
interview.

Her name was Ann. She
would soon meet my father, and
get pregnant with me.
The gardener's name was Frank.
He was not supposed to be outside. He
had knocked an orderly unconscious and
taken his keys.

You know, this joke isn't really
that funny. It's not really a joke
at all. Thank God she was not hurt badly –
scared mostly.
I suppose Dad wouldn't have
told the joke at all if
he'd gone to college instead
of her.

Day 1

I woke up on Day 1 and
held my wife for the first time,
drank tea for the first time,
saw my first snow, all before
6:30.
My story? I was born at 5:45 when
the alarm went off. I spent my
childhood showering and shaving and
here I am; no scars, no
nightmares, no scores to
settle.
Is it always this windy? I
have a job, I
assume I'll know what to do
when I get there. I don't
know what I'll wear, or
eat. My wife's name is
Susan, she's very
nice.

Day 1

I was born at 5:45 to the
sound of a bell. I grew
up in a blue bathroom with
yellow light and steam. As a
young man I fed cats and made
lunches. Here I am, in my prime;
writing in my journal, getting ready for
the outdoors, a walk to work, coffee.
It is gray and cold outside and
that is fine too. There is a lovely woman
drinking tea – I remember her from being
birthed from the bed. Outside birds sort
seeds in a copper feeder. On the rug a
small gray animal makes a sound like
a diesel. The heat just clicked on. I am
in love with this brand new life.

Day 1

I was born early, struggling
up through the muck like a crazed
tadpole, too soon, anything to escape that
weird pre-birth dream. I'm a twin, but my brother is
somehow trapped in my skull, cramped and angry,
suggesting the most vulgar and preposterous things
in a way that makes my brain spin like a motorcycle on
a frozen lake. Can I get a do-over, can I crawl back
into the flannel womb? I've come out in the wrong
world, this one is not safe or friendly.

Day 1

Everything appears brand new – some things
are still warm to the touch. I am
brand new. I feel inclined to write a poem, but
what can I write about, as I have never wept, or
had my heart broken, or experienced death or
fear or shame? I don't even know
words for the things I see and hear and smell.
Just as well – why bother with descriptions of a
thing, when the thing is
right there? Why run to get a pen and paper to
write a clumsy account of a sunrise, when I'll
miss some of it in the process?
Better to just
pay attention.
The sky looks like murder, bloody and bruised
a beautiful thing
a beautiful thing
trees cut from black paper, stiff and unused
the sky is a
beautiful thing.
I couldn't help it.

Day 1

Tired.
My head feels so thick, like my

blood is maple syrup being pushed through
human hair veins, I'm suffocating in my own
head.
Mark my words, one day someone
is going to crack open my head and find a
black egg, a large jewel, a rope tied
in a knot, a brain half turned to coral, and
we will all go "a-HA."
That being said, there is a beautiful
light in the sky, turning those huge
streaks glorious colors.

Day 1

Everything is dark, except for
the small glow of a bedside lamp. The
day is over. It was a good day – I did what
I set out to do. Susan, my partner, my
love throughout this long day, is already
gone to sleep. It is time to close my eyes.
Black boat,
black water,
black sand.

Divine Wind

Men turned themselves into
human arrows, a sacrifice for
honor, country,
outcome.
Now, a kamikaze is
a cocktail for
college girls.
Sometime soon frat
boys on the
town will order
Suicide Bomber shots
at the bar.
To forget, or
remember?

Dog as Poet

I watched the dog kicking at
his belly, as if trying to
open his own underside,
set something free.
I wanted to help him,
to ease his pain, but
he snapped and howled and
wouldn't let me near him.
It was as if he had swallowed a
bucket of
seeds that were
shooting out tendrils in his
gut, threatening to explode him, and the
only way to survive was
to tear himself
open.

Drums along the Interstate

When I was just a little boy-boy-boy
my family lived in a house with highway sounds
sometimes my Pop was unemploy-ploy-ployed
sometimes my sisters and my brother were not around
sometimes I'd run off through the tree-tree-trees
and watch all of those cars, some fast, some slow
on Route Ninety-three-three-Three
that's when I realized I had to find a place to go
I used to have bad dreams-dreams-dreams
and moments of blinding numbing joy
I couldn't hide the sloppy seams-seams-seams
I had no skin, too many feelings for a boy
I used to listen to the Who-Who-Who
and Eric Clapton, Bruce Springsteen and the Rolling Stones
I smoked dope and drank boo-boo-booze
I was a vandal and a dreamer and I felt alone
sometimes I used to cut my skin-skin-skin
sometimes I'd break things just to hear the sound
you see, I already had sinned, sinned, sinned
there was no point in trying to hold the higher ground
the sound of tires in the rain-rain-rain
punctured my heart and made me want to cry
there was no way I could explain-ain-ain
the way my wires got crossed, the way the sparks could fly
I felt uncomfortable at schoo-schoo-school
I was an underachiever, lousy sense of self
but this left me free to choo-choo-choose
a different path from everybody else
I heard the music in my head-head-head
a fucked-up radio with a busted dial
I heard every word they said-said-said
I found a brand new way to exhort and defile
a fifty-dollar Guild guitar-tar-tar
I met a girl and we started acting like adults
man, I was gonna be a star-star-star
I was gonna get results results results
and still I'd run off through the tree-tree-trees
and I'd dream of going places I didn't even know
on Route Ninety-three-three-Three
didn't want to live in my skin, no more, no more.

that's where the story ends for now-now-now
a hill at dusk above the Interstate
having a smoke and wondering how-how-how
you shake the feeling that you're always one day late.

Everything

Where does this
crap come from?
Lean years, hard times, cold
climates, family sadness?

"Don't ask
for
too much."

Listen –
If you let the
feast go
un-tasted, you
miss an opportunity and
disrespect the
Chef.

Go on.
Taste.
Eat.
Ask
for
Everything.

Fear®

If you don't please your
parents you will be
abandoned.

If you do not have the right
shape, or healthy shiny hair you will not
find love.

If you do not prepare the right
meals your family will slowly
reject you.

If you do not take the right medicines you
will live a life not much better than
death.

If you do not drive a large enough car your
family will perish in the horrible accident
that will most surely occur.

If you allow two people of the same
gender to be married in your community,
your children, (most certainly their children)

will end up gay and miserable, and God
(your God, the One God,) will be
furious.

If we do not crush people we do not
understand, they will
slit our throats in our
sleep.

If you disagree with me then
you are a
coward and a
sneak.

Fear.
It makes a country great.

(Unless, of course, something goes terribly wrong...)

Folk Song Hero

I never knew the man.
But then again neither did you, nor
anyone who has sung that
damn song. You know, the
one about that fine fearsome
Jesse James, his sweet wife, his brave
children.

Did that coward Robert Ford shoot
him in the back while Jesse hung
a picture on the wall? Yes he did.
Know why? Because Jesse was an
unpredictable psychopath. Was ol'
Robert a coward? You bet. A fool?
Not entirely.

The song suggests that no man was
tough enough to take him one-on-one;
of course we'll never know, because
Jesse surrounded himself with
a gang. Brave Jesse.

How bad should we feel for his
wife? She married this
thug who couldn't or wouldn't work
like everyone else – all he was good for was
taking things that didn't belong to him and
terrorizing people.

Poor Jesse. Couldn't keep the
Civil War going forever. Pissed off
the locals by
stealing their money.
Shot by one of the losers he
recruited. Golly, it's like a
Greek tragedy!

Don't get me wrong –
I dig songs about bold deeds and
fallen heroes, I just don't know

any folk songs about the
Indians. Just this myth about an
ignorant thief.

And history shall record how
that coward Robert Ford
laid poor Jesse in his grave.

Four Days in November

One
and the day came up golden
and the sky bright blue steel
and the wood rough and sun-warm
and the coffee hot, bitter
and the day fresh-baked bread
and the day un-locked trunk
and the day sharp horizon
and the day wild horse.

Two
and the day came up hidden
and the sky aluminum
and the air a cold whisper
and the gray wrapped around us
and the day blank paper
and the day ringing phone
and the day unopened book
and the day circling hawk

Three
and the heater runs, panting
and the memories frozen clothesline
and the air cold clean metal
and the sky blueberry parfait
and the day a curved road
and the day stacked wood
and the day thirteen dollars
and the day a door ajar.

Four
and the sun climbs the barn roof
and sits burning golden
and the streets lifeless ribbon
and the wind gentle broom
and the day sleeping dog
and the day boiling kettle
and the day pen on paper
and the stones cold and still.

Genius

Lab, I think.
Maybe black. Maybe mutt, I
don't know. I do remember the
woman, not what she looked like, but
what she did. She sat in a low
beach chair as the sun went down and
the tide went up, a paperback in
one hand and a tennis racquet
in the other. Either it was a kick-ass book, or
she was worn out, as she barely looked up
at the nodding boats or the
hammered gold bay.
But the dog!
The dog was on fire and had to
throw himself in the ocean again and
again, eyes with that mad
insistence, cords of muscle like
suspender straps.
He would bring her the tennis ball
as if her life depended on it, a
heroic act and she, with bored detachment,
would serve that ball hundreds of feet
into the bay.
Look at him go! A wet-fur missile, a genius
of retrieval, a tireless fetching machine.
Again.
Again.
He was Ali, she was Foreman, hitting with
all her strength, trying, no doubt, to tire
him out and only inching closer to surrender.
He would have fetched until his
heart burst. If he had a voice he
would have laughed, and whooped.
I watched him with awe, with reverence,
with envy, this creature who was doing
exactly what he was
put here to do and finding
such joy in it.

get ready

Listen –
we've allowed ourselves to be
snake-charmed, lulled, we've
balanced the bowling ball of
our beliefs on the knitting needle tip of wishful thinking.
We are overdrawn, and
under-prepared, we've buttered our bread and
made our beds and the
Peterbuilt of Reckoning is
grinding up the far side of a
near hill.
The roller coaster car is
clack-clack-clacking to the
top of that first heart-stopping drop and
-by the way, they never finished
building the tracks.

What am I talking about?
I'll tell you what I'm talking about.
An event is going to happen that will make
Revelations look like a
Disney movie, make the
Four Horsemen look like the
Three Amigos.

Someday
Keith Richards is
going to die, and when he does you'd
better be ready; you'd better pray to
your God or Higher Power that you rely on
because the transitory and impermanent nature
of Life will be revealed as the
sputtering birthday candle that
it is.
When Keef, our Dorian Gray, the
king of the un-dead becomes
un-un-dead, then we can count on
<u>nothing.</u>

Water will flow uphill,

ice will burn,
gravity will turn sideways,
cats will mate with dogs,
things will cost what they're worth,
liars will not prosper,
fairness and common sense will be the
law of the land.

In short,
utter
madness.

the Glass

...and the glass
literally
leapt out of my
hand, as if the glass was
warm Teflon and my fingers were
slick with Vaseline, or WD-40, or
blood: it shot, as if
propelled away from me,
as if it were a space capsule blasting
away from its booster rocket, as if the
glass and my hand were made of powerful
opposing magnets, as if we
stood before a black hole that sucked
the glass into its vortex –
I may have been tired, but I was
dead sober, and I'm telling
you that that glass was like a
terrified living thing that had to escape my
grasp in order to save its own life.
It
literally
leapt out of my hand, as if my
hand were a greased flipper, and
it lifted out of my hand as if
we were in zero gravity, and I'm
standing there, watching this glass turning slowly like
a moon in space; I can see what it
will hit, how it will bounce to the
tile floor and shatter; I see my
bare feet, I see the whole kitchen floor and where
every shard will land, I hear my wife's
voice rising with alarm; the
stitches, the mismatched set, I
sit home while she takes walks
further and further away...
and then there's this spasm, this jolt, like a
tic really, and the glass is in my hand; faster than
I could think it my hand caught the
glass and is holding it like a father
holds a newborn, like it was a sticky orange, safe,

amazing.
everything's fine, as if it never really happened.
It never happened.
It never happened.

Goliath

In the dream I stood with strangers around
a camp fire. The rest of the tribe, exhausted and beat,
camped in the darkness.

"They have a champion," the King said, with some effort,
"And we have no one..." All eyes were on the ground.
A moment of silence crawled by.

"King?" I said, "if there's one thing I can't stand it's a
damn bully." I called out,
"Can anyone here use a grindstone?"

A hand went up cautiously. I took the useless sword off the
King's bony hip. "Sharpen this like a razor, both sides."
Eyes lifted.
"Tomorrow I'm going to cut someone's goddam head off."

In the morning I drank coffee black, and said 'no thanks' to
the armor. "It ain't going to last that long." Down into the
valley I marched,
towards the silhouette of their champion.

"Don't look so big," I mumbled, cutting
the humid air into ribbons.
"Don't look so tough."

Their champion stood in the sand, wearing polyester slacks
and a
'World's #1 Grandma' sweatshirt, the sun glinting off her
bifocals.
"We had such high hopes for you," she sighed.

My guts turned to ice cream. I cocked the sword like a
baseball bat,
feeling the eyes of the King and his army on my back.
"It's a good thing your father isn't here to see this..."

Back at camp no one said a word. That night the
King politely asked for his sword back.
"Everyone has an off day," I grumbled.

In the morning I drank whiskey and snarled at my comrades. I marched into
the valley and came face-to-face with a four-year old in cowboy pajamas, his hair cut in crooked bangs that accentuated his big ears.

He had a toy sword made from a fence picket. I tightened my grip on my blade and
he began to cry.
"For Christ's sake, knock that off!"

Now he really began to wail.
A dark stain spread from his crotch.
Back at camp we talked about everything but.

The next morning, I left camp before anyone awoke, my shame
burning in me like a wick in a lamp. I had been tricked, humiliated.
I ran to the valley. It wouldn't happen again.

I came face to face with myself.
"That does it!" I said.
"That does it," he said.
"Games over!" I said.
"Games over," he said.
"Keep it up, asshole!" I said.
"Keep it-"

His head came off with a sound like chopping a bunch of celery, and rolled
in the dirt. I listened for the cheers, and
realized there wouldn't be
any.
Alone in the
hot
morning and
I couldn't
wake
up.

Gratitude II

thank you for the church bell
in a sky smeared red like blood
thank you for the gunshot
that ricochets through the night
car radio playing the Family Stone
rain in the gutter
a whisper, a flutter
thank you for the church bell
in a sky smeared red like blood

Thank you for the barking dog
chewing a hole in the dark
thank you for the suspicious wind
that makes leaves dance and attack
the ghosts of the past walk ahead on the road
a moan, a murmur
a glint a glimmer
thank you for the barking dog
chewing a hole in the dark

thank you for the children
locked in an attic room
thank you for the fever-dreams
of giants, angels and fire
the crippling straps, the telescopes
a promise spoken
a mirror broken
thank you for the children
locked in an attic room

Healthy Outlook

I ♥ my chemicals.
I ♥ my mood swings.
I don't have a dog, or
children in a school, so my
bumper sticker options are
limited.
I ♥ lifting depression.
I ♥ those days when I can see it
coming and get into my three-point
stance, I ♥ when it blows past me like a
tornado that miraculously missed the
house, I ♥ waking up in my own bed, no
bruises, wallet on the dresser, car in
the driveway, no memory of the
preceding night, no harm done.
I ♥ the crowbar of
gratitude tearing off the boards
nailed over the window.
I ♥ the will to live.
I ♥ opening my eyes.
It's a brand new day.
It's always a brand new day.

I ♥ that.

How to Tend a Fire

Most of the time it
takes care of
itself.

It's all about hunger and
fuel and gravity.
Most of the time it
settles as it should.

The key is to
be sure that everything
gets an opportunity
to burn, that

nothing goes to
waste, that it is
hot and
bright and
gets
enough
air.

I am the Product of a Transistor Radio

I.
I got a girl named
Bony Maronie, I got a girl named Rama
Lama Ding Dong, I got a woman 'way
cross town, come on down to my boat baby
let's play house of the rising sun catch
you crying over you better move on the poor
side of town without pity can do the
wah-watusti on South Street fighting man man's
world without love potion #9 #9 #99 tears of
a clown, downtown, shop around, I found
a love me do you want to know
a secret agent man who shot
Liberty Valance? This could be the last
time is on my side of the road runner
baby let's play house.

II.
I hear you knockin' but you can't
come in the still of the night time has come today
I met the boy from New York City little
bitty pretty one-two-three red light my fire on
the mountain of love me tender is the night train
to Memphis Tennessee.

III.
Meanwhile, back in the States...

IV.
The last thing I remember, Doc, I started to pony, to twist, the mashed potato, the swim, the monkey, the Freddie, the slop, the hucklebuck, the boomerang, the peppermint twist, the clam, the bird, the jerk, the New Continental, the funky chicken...

V.
My Pop said "son you gonna drive me to
drinkin' if you don't stop driving that hot
fun in the summer time of the season of the witch
way you goin' Billy don't be a heroes and villains."

Ooh baby baby lets play house party
lights baby lets play the game of
love on a two-way down yonder in
New York groove me baby let's play
house of blue's theme from a
summer in the city.

VI.
And so on, and so on, and scoobie doobie do.

I couldn't sleep

I couldn't sleep because I
couldn't breathe. I
did not dream. I
woke up exhausted.

To run the
marathon of each day I
drank coffee going uphill,
smoked cigarettes going
down.

In the evening more
caffeine to try to
write, the words like
chicks on a
hotplate.

I wore my life like
an ill-fitting
suit.

At night my heart
like a jazz drummer's
snare, worries were bats
pressing against the windows.
Sparks and smoke from the
fuse box.

The drinks saved me and
I fell in love with
the lifeguard.

What looked like a large
vodka tonic was in fact a
large vodka.
ditto
ditto

I gained weight. I
did not like the

doughiness, but
after a life of feeling small it was
intriguing to appear
big.

I couldn't sleep because I
couldn't breathe. I
did not dream. I
woke up exhausted.

My wife, also unable to
sleep would shake me awake and
whisper "Stop! You're
doing it again!"

I wanted to weep –
I had no idea what I
was doing, except I had
just fallen asleep.

All my life.
Stop – you're doing it again.

I couldn't sleep because I
couldn't breathe. I
did not dream. I woke up
exhausted.

They wired me from
head to toe; strange, bored
science fiction. I sat in the
attic looking like a
broken television,
drinking.
For accuracy.

The data suggested that
I was dying little deaths
in my sleep.
Not the French kind.
Quite the opposite.
No dreams.

My heart was a fairly new car with
too many miles on it.

The apparatus turned me into
a nightmare pachyderm. The
hum, the tangle, the constant wind
in my face.
Now I had dreams.
Bad dreams.

The doctor broke my
nose and stuffed my head with
cotton. I got
four days off from
work.

I woke up tired. I
cried in the shower, my
prayers to make through
another day sounding
pitiful.

Drinks and
cigarettes were my
Christmas and
Birthday.

Desperation can make you do
foolish things.
Exhaustion can make you
turn away from the one who
truly loves you.
I placed my false peace in
a paper boat and
put it in the stream.

And now I sleep.
and now I dream.
And sometimes I dream of
whiskey.
And sometimes I dream of

wine.
And sometimes I dream of
me, in the paper boat,
taking on water.

I'll give you something to cry about...

Mom?
Dad?
Look at me.
I'm not even four years old.
You are upset about something I
don't understand and I'm
scared. You should see your faces – you
look like crazy people.

I live in a house full of
giants. I can't
do anything for myself. I can't
answer your questions, I can't
explain myself, I can't even
tell you what I was trying
to do. All I can do is stand here reaching
for you, crying.

Your heartache is grown-up heartache:
rejected by a lover, job lost, death of a parent,
withering of a
dream –
you've forgotten the primal terror of being
so small
so helpless
so unsafe
in danger of not being loved.

Do you see why
I'm confused?
I've clearly already got
something to
cry about.

Jazz

I really should
like jazz – not just
the cliché of it; the pork pie hats and
basement clubs and reefer and secret
language, although you'd think I'd
like all that;

but you'd think I would like the
structured chaos of those drunken melodies that
rush, blindfolded, up and down the stairs, the
detachment, the rejection of all that is
Popular and surefire,

the quiet pride of standing apart, the
respect for tradition,
the disdain for tradition, the
soft danger of it.

But the truth is that for the most part I
can't bear it; it moves like a bird, not enough
weight, so hard to follow, too many
songs played too many times.

It withholds clues, it rolls its eyes at you, it
suggests exclusion, it's like my high school
guidance counselor who, oblivious that I had to
try harder than most just to keep up said that I
just don't try hard enough.

Fuck that.
At least Rock & Roll says
What the hell, come on in, there's always room for
one more.

JC w/ ADD

I see that train a rollin', it's
rolling on its back, and
I ain't seen the sunshine since the
dawn was just a crack, but
time it keeps a-draggin', I'm
in this prison still, and
that train just keeps a-rollin' to
the bottom of the hill.

When I was just a baby my
mama told me "John,
always take the gloves off and
keep the blinders on", but
I shocked a man named Nero, just
to watch him fry, and when
I hear that train a-tumblin', I
forget my alibi.

It sounds like rich folks floppin' in
a fancy drinking car, no
way to smoke that coffee, or
eat them big cigars, but
I know I had it coming, so
they put the hammer down, and
those jumbled-up folk are wondering, which
way's the sky, which
way's the ground?

If they freed me from this prison if
that railroad train was mine, I'd
put it back together with an
arc-welder, and twine, I'd
point it towards Waukegan, I'd
make that fire roar, and
I wouldn't stop for nothin', and I'd
nail shut all the doors.

I'd scream through all the crossings and
I wouldn't touch the brakes, I'd
wail that lonesome whistle and keep

everyone awake, I'd
head straight for the ocean, I'd
lash myself to the wheel, and
way down at the bottom I'd finally
rest these bones and steel.

Jerry Lee

Rock stars these days
behave badly; drink
too much, drug
too much, treat their girlfriends
like shit, give photographers
the finger.

Now, Jerry Lee said
"Yes Sir" and "No sir" and
set his piano on fire and
married his 15 year old
cousin and
told the world to
screw.

Beat that.

Joy Wins

Joy wins like this:
five minutes of sitting on
the deck in the morning sun,
coffee, chaos of birdsong, first
motorcycle of the season, no
coat, no socks, sweet breeze with
ocean and wood smoke, five minutes
of this and the sleet and metal sky, the
slush and thick coats, the
dirty cars and short days
disappear.
Waiting is replaced with
possibility. All is
uncovered. A million
tiny green miracles.
Joy wins like
this.

Letter to Khrushchev

If I'd been JFK I would have
said:

Go ahead, make as many missiles as you want,
put them in Cuba, put them on
Martha's damn Vineyard for all I care, paint them bright
red and put horrible stingers on their tips, put my
children's pictures on each and
every one, you cannot possibly be so stupid as to actually
fire one of those things.
You put all your money into Flying Death Machines
too big to use, fine; eat turnips and drive crap cars
if it makes you feel big.
No more missiles for us, thanks, we've
got plenty. Instead I'm going to buy
every man, woman and child in America some good
books, an excellent bicycle, a full toolbox
from Sears, a pair of new sneakers, the musical
instrument of their choice, and a year's worth of ice cream
and we'll see who buries who.

like a whip

my spine is fused with worry
like a chain with welded links -
the hatches have been bolted shut
the air is thick and stale
the generator is winding down
the lights an amber glow
everything is rust

it literally hurts to think
swimming through oil,
my skull a faulty pressure-cooker
my eyes hot grapes
I am disinterested in myself
the sparkling water in my head
has been replaced with cooling lava
the music replaced with the whine
and groan of shifting ice, old
appliance hum, the sizzle of grease in a
hot pan.

Please
take me by my ankles and
crack me like a whip
beat me like a rug, boil me in
clean water and fling me
out over the falls; stretch
me on a hot rock to dry, to be
eaten by crows and shat out over the ocean where
 I can be re-formed, re-birthed, re-evolved into some
sightless fish that crawls up on the beach
and grows legs, ready for a
new day.

Love

How do I love thee?
More than this –
I love you cross-eyed
delirium and soft longing, scraped
raw and butterfly kissed, after
the fight and across a
crowded room, damp from the
shower or dusted with
flour, I love you the
long train of days and the
shock of recognition, I
love you with need and
generosity, I love you the
mirror and the horizon, inside and
outside, I love you the quiet heartbreak
of the last day, and two
Ss in a warm bed.

Lover Overheard

I overheard my
lover talking to her
friends at a party. She said
"There's a right way and a
wrong way. I always light two red
candles and brush my teeth. Kissing and
touching should only last as long as two short songs or
one long one. I sing 'I Can't Stand the Rain' in my
head and moan on the word 'rain'.
I move my feet in small circles like
I'm pedaling a bike. Back-arching or hair-pulling
are fine, but not both. Near the end I make my eyes
very wide and hold my breath. Sometimes I
pretend I hear someone outside the
door."

I felt the same way when I
read those essays the poet wrote
about writing
poetry.
I didn't need to know that shit.
I thought I was
discovering something.

Lucinda Williams, How Could You?

Like it wasn't enough
to bust in on me at
work, obviously drunk, and
tear open your blouse,
suggesting that I cut out your
heart right then, with Mrs. Hardy's
letter opener, as I had turned it
into a dead and useless thing by
denying you my love.

Like you couldn't simply
scrawl those mad, lurid
messages on my windshield
with your unmistakable
lipstick, or howl outside
my apartment, burning my letters in
a champagne bucket until
the cops come.

I almost miss you
standing outside the
restaurant window
slowly eating an apple by
cutting it into slivers with
a long knife, or those phone messages at
all hours when you would, in your
ragged whisper say
"You belong to *me*!" over
and over.

I thought it was over. I
never imagined that you were
so bitter that you would find this
new way to twist me up
by pretending that we've
never met, while singing
every new song
to
me.

My Love

Sometimes
I'm fine with my space
and solitude – in fact
I crave them, but
other times (like right now) I
want to cling to you like
we're on the run from the
law, and they're chasing us with
dogs, and we're holding
each other in a swamp, under-
water, breathing through straws,
fierce partners hanging on
until the danger is
past.

New Motto

I have a new motto. I have
tattooed it on the insides of my
eyelids, I have carved it into

the old oak tree in the Town
Square, I have named my yacht
after it, I have hung from a rope and

chiseled it into the rock face, I
have sewed tags into my clothes, I
have added it to the choruses of

songs, I have spelled it out with
flowers in the rock garden, I have
drawn it on my sleeping lover's skin with

kisses, I have welded it onto the
side of a barge, I've painted it on the
town water tower, I've embroidered it

on an heirloom sampler, I've hired a
skywriter to emblazon it on
the blue over my head:

Enjoy.

New Voice

A hammer head broken from
its handle becomes, what?
A paperweight? That's a
far cry from building
houses, bud.

A bird is perfection as
a flying machine, but break its
wing and it becomes some
stray cats terrified meal.

What do you do when
you spend your life as
one thing, and then you
lose it?

Ask the painter whose
eyes cloud over, the
trumpeter with the
busted lip, the
window washer who grows
afraid of heights.

What do you do when
your linkage rusts solid, when
your map shows places that
no longer exist?

It can feel like
Change is trying to
snap your leg, but
it's really trying to
save your ass.

So maybe you accept the
gifts of the unknown, of
exploration, maybe you
find your
new voice.

Not Going Back

My favorite place was
the abandoned power station –
the thousand rusted spears
of the iron fence, the
ruin of better days, the
smokestack that gave
the city the finger
all day, every day.

The housing projects
all had English-novel
names: Cottage Place Gardens, Mulford
Gardens, Jesus
Christ.
Some neighbors once stabbed a
thief in the ass so
he'd have to sit and
wait for the cops.
Pit bull puppies died
chained to
radiators.

Everything was a
consolation prize that
didn't console.
Colored plastic, flashing
lights, the biggest, cheapest
sandwich, something stolen,
not because it was a bargain, but
because
Fuck You Too,
Jack.

of course

of course we drink, we were born to drink, we were put on this earth with a twisted leg, too broken to fly and too proud to beg, a thief's bravado, a tinker's dam, a knockout punch but a spun-glass jaw, a rule book soaked in gasoline, a big broken heart with a sucking wound, a funeral smirk and a wang dang doodle, a smoker's hack, a nod and a wink,
of course we drink,
we were born to drink.

of course we lie, we were born to lie, we arrive here wired to invent and create, we spin elegant webs and then it's too late, it's fiction, it's friction, the truth's too plain, the original language is the one we use, weaving colorful fabric with no thread on the spool, everything's possible, give it a shot, why settle for something that's just not enough, the original alchemists, reckless and flawed, daring to break what we've been told is law, it's just not enough to be born and then die, so
of course we lie,
we were put here to lie.

of course we steal, we were made to steal, put here with a hunger that's never sated, our dreams are tin, those others gold-plated, we're just righting the scales, so wrongfully tipped, because unfairness festers, unfairness infests, it must be addressed so we give ourselves gifts because someone forgot, and the world's in grave danger if we can't love ourselves, it's all there on the shelves just waiting for us, why shame ourselves with requests and appeals,
of course we steal,
we were made to steal.

of course we drink, we were born to lie, we steal from the clock and we steal from death, we lie to ourselves about our need to drink, and we drink to forget the lies and the theft, we steal to drink and we drink to lie and we lie to explain to a dangerous world that to steal is simply to move a thing, that a lie's a creation, a poem, a game, and to drink is to let

God's tears drop on your tongue, with broken fingers we
reach towards the light,
so of course we write,
of course we write.

Old Man

the old man
did not approve
of the cat
and had little
to do with
it until he
read that petting
an animal lowered
one's blood pressure
which he found,
astonishingly,
to be true.

He even discovered
that when he
rubbed the old
cat's paws his
own arthritic hands
were soothed.

So what could
they do when
they found him
that night curled
on the floor
tears running down
his worn cheeks
kissing the old
sleeping cat and
whispering "It's not
your fault, it
was never your
fault."

Our Original Purpose

So there's this Roman
Emperor, I forget his name, and he's done
pretty well for himself
but he's getting old, and the shine is
off him, and he knows that nothing gets people's
attention like a war.

He says "those Caledonians are a bunch of
wild men, and until we defeat them we'll never really
be safe." It didn't matter that these Caledonians
were in the Scottish Highlands and
didn't give a boar's ass about Rome.
Still.

So he moves his whole operation to
York, England, and he gets his toughest boys from
all over, and they start burning Caledonian villages and
killing everything that moves.

Now, the Roman have the numbers, and the
technology – they are the Super Power. Of course,
the pissed-off Caledonian in the bushes with the club
could care less. These fancy pigs have killed his
family, and they're going to pay.

And they do.
It turns out that stealth and ambush and bitterness and
home-field advantage work pretty well
against a Super Power.

I was going to call this poem Humans Don't Learn
Shit From History, but I didn't want to be vulgar.

I wonder if
God looks down
and bangs his fist on his
forehead and mutters,
"come *on*!", or
if this is all actually
fine, as our original

purpose is to supply the
earth with
much-needed
fertilizer?

Picking a Fight with a New Yorker

Don't give me that
look like you don't know.

You *don't* know, do you!

Who did you think stole
your car, with it's fancy
burglar alarm? And that fire next
door, that started all by its
self? Who did you think drove over
your new grass, who did you think left that
whiskey bottle in your mailbox, who did
you think was clipping your prize
roses, and who did you think put your
Doberman in that
ballerina outfit?

Listen.
Every Tuesday night, when your
girl says she's "out with her
sister"?

Come on.
It's been the Boston
Red Sox the whole
time.

Poems for Restless Children #7

The Road to Hell is paved with bricks
the telegraph wire is strung on sticks
the sidewalk's strewn with glass and nails
the trolley rolls on bones for rails.

The sky is red, the air is foul
the hounds are mute, the rabbits howl
leaky roofs and rotted floors
and always room for just one more.

There's neighborhoods where you will find
the damned must live with their own kind
what punishment could be more true,
than eternity with someone just like you?

Cheats and bullies grub for trash
the unkind wrestle cans of ash
and hand-in-hand down in the pit
the self-righteous and the hypocrite.

Poem Notes

She does
this and I
do that –
I notice how something reminds me
of something else. I
evoke a sort of quiet
sadness when I describe the stray flower
pushing up through the
gravel, the Jeep with a
broken spring, a rusted folding chair
caught forty feet up
in a tree, tiny fingers
drawing in the fog of a
school bus window.
My father has been
dead for eleven
years. I want to write
a poem but I have to
go to work.

Remembering Carl

Ah, Carl
you were as dumb as an
anvil, one could practically see
the thoughts plodding from
one part of your brain to
another, like an elderly man trying to
cross a busy avenue carrying a
heavy box.
Good God, you were thick, you
made Jethro Bodean look like a
city slicker. Remember that time
you decided you wanted to talk to the audience
so you called out, "Hey everybody –
what's your name?"
You were dumb and petty, even
if you did have a good
heart in that powerful chest.
Your mom was worse – she was
dumb and nasty. At least you could be
cheery.
But here's the thing – it didn't
matter, not a spec, and in your
way you were a better man than
I, because you were a great drummer,
born with a welterweight's arms and
a clock in your head. You could make
your snare drum bark like a big
dog, your kick drum
was a thunderclap. You could
swing, by god, and play complicated
rhythms by ear.
That's all I wanted to say.
That and the part about your
mom being dumb
and mean.

Rough Tuesday

of course it's
the coffee, the
fucking coffee, and
the rain.
it's just the rain and the coffee, and
the job is still new so
it takes some time to
get used to it, right?
it's just the
rain and the bad
wiring, like a bird's nest of
old frayed lamp cord, you
pour a couple of cups of
coffee on that mess and the
sparks fly.
and the smell? like
a fluorescent ballast gone
bad, like a fire in a
used tire yard, enough rain to
soak your pants and shoes, but
not enough to put out that son of a
gun.
it's just the depression, you
know that, it comes and goes like
arthritis – the fucking rain!
you're down, you're up, don't
sweat it, it's bearable.
the coffee doesn't
help, by the way. it shines a light
in your eyes, it makes you grind your
teeth, you take deep breaths like you're
out of breath, what's that?
so you cried, so what?
nobody saw. it's the damn
rain, how can you not feel
helpless in this weather?
you're tired and jacked up and damp and resigned.
don't you see? it's
the coffee.
and the damn

rain.

Something Must Be Done

I read somewhere that there are
more writers of poetry than readers of poetry.
Or maybe that more books of poetry were being

written than bought. Either way it troubled me enormously.
Can't you see where it will lead? It will be worse than
L.A. waiters with screenplays – poets will break into

houses to leave chapbooks on
nightstands, poets will haul unsuspecting
pedestrians down filthy

alleys and shove them roughly to their
knees and hiss "Read it! Slow!"
Poets in rags, on corners, in

subway cars, sitting on collapsed
boxes chanting "I'm not on drugs and I don't
steal – I just want you to read my sonnet."

Why?

Why do people want to be
poets? Poets don't get cool nicknames, like
Sylvia "Lady Despair" Plath, or Jack

"The Typewriter" Kerouac, Billy "Catfish" Collins, or
Langston "Duke" Hughes.
When was the last time you read about a

poet getting pulled over in his
sports car, drunk with an underage
Ecuadorian beauty? Doing community service time for

belting a paparazzi?
Exactly. Never.
Worn out sweaters, full ashtrays, postage receipts.

Listen up, people – we are crowded into a
under-sized lifeboat with one package of

saltines. It's time to be noble, it's time for
heroism. So the tribe can survive.

First; stop writing poetry.
Then, buy my book – why should we all perish?
Don't do it for me, or even for yourself...do it
in the memory of Ezra "the Godfather of Modernism,
PoetBrother Number 1" Pound.

String Theory

Thousands of lives are being
spent trying to construct an
Explanation of Everything, six

extra dimensions, parallel universes,
the whole overloaded wagon held
together with tiny bits of string.

String?

Why not tiny jacks, or tiny crescent
wrenches or tiny dandelions, or tiny
charm bracelets, or tiny umbrellas, or

tiny teacups, or tiny disco balls, or
tiny rubber bands, paper clips?
Our Universe is as it is because of

tiny hoops of twine? This
is what you get from too much
coffee and a 'what if' –

When my friends and I considered
such possibilities behind the
cafeteria with a nickel bag of

lame weed, it did not occur
to us that we were budding physicists;
we were burnouts
trying to get comfortable with

mystery.

Texas

Pop was in
Texas for the Gemini
launch. I
was a four-year old running
through the sprinkler in
Massachusetts.
Pop sent postcards that said that
it was so hot down there that
people even had air-conditioning
in their cars.
I sent Pop a postcard of
Fenway Park that was a real
45 that played "Take me out
to the ballgame."
Pop helped hurl a
man beyond Earth's
gravity, and worried that he
might have to move his family
away from the neighbors they'd
just met.
I wondered if he'd
bring me a present and why
he was staying so long in this
hot place called
Texas.

Thank God for Friends

You draw a picture of
a dog you had as
a child.

You show it to someone, who,
remembering their childhood dog says
"the ears should be bigger."

Someone else, who used to
watch a lot of Lassie, says that if only the
fur was longer, it would be a good picture
of a dog.

Someone else who is allergic to dogs, but
likes cats suggests that it
would look good with whiskers.

Someone who was
bitten by a dog says
"Ugh – why not do a still life of
fruit?"

Someone who went to art school says
"your representation is simplistic and
the light is all wrong."

A neighbor asks if you
think it will sell.

A guy at work insists in
showing you all of his
sketches.

Your childhood friend says, "Will
you look at that – it's Duke."

That's the one

What do you call that feeling,
when you are looking out into
the distance, especially from up on a high
outcropping of
some kind, looking out over a
large body of water, a distant
horizon, and you are looking intently
over a great distance, not really focusing on
one object, looking to see
what's coming, and also not looking
outside yourself, scanning both the
inner and outer horizons, feeling
anxious for something to appear, so
you can gauge it, feeling restless, but also
somewhat rooted to where you
stand, lost, for that moment in
Time, independent of all things but
a part of all things, lonely and safe, wanting
everything and nothing at
the same time, what do you call
that feeling?

Because that's how I feel.

The Kiss

The moment of anticipation is
part of the magic. It's like standing on the high
diving board, waiting for absolute stillness. There is
the certainty that a beautiful natural thing
is about to take place.

A thick short glass with
dew forming on the outside. Ice cubes that
look like huge raw diamonds
that have had their edges softened by the gentle
persistent flow of a stream.

The glass is filled with color, with
longing. The color is like old copper, like
autumn leaves in a rain barrel, like
honey. The longing is for peace.

Then, the kiss.

Electric eels swim on the tongue.
The tears of an Indian Princess.
The piss of angels on Valentines Day.

A rough warm
snake crawls to the belly. Sherman's gentle
March to the Sea. Scottish lava
lovingly destroys Pompeii.
God's bitter love.
The Miracle Solvent coats the rusty machinery. The
heart isn't just beating, it's playing the
drum riff to 'Be My Baby' by the
Ronettes.

Hurt is put in perspective. Faults are
forgivable. Every song is your song.
Hope is an option.

I am handsome, and at ease.

Another double, please.

Woodshed

He'd been in bands where
his lightning
spider-walk
fretwork had
made the amphetamine crowd
howl.
They wanted speed and
electricity and
he gave it to them.

But one night
on the way home he
saw some of them transfixed
by a burning building, and
when the plate-glass exploded, they
howled
just like they did for his
lightning
spider-walk
fretwork.

So now he sits in
a dim small room
teaching himself to play that
one note, slowly, perfectly
over and over.

Workbench

His workbench was Jules
Verne, and Thomas Edison and
your nutty Uncle Earle, Santa if
he was drunk. It was an artful chaos
of hardened tubes of goo, potentiometers,
cotter pins in baby food
jars, 12AX7 tubes, homemade
jigs, handles without sockets, sockets
without handles, one-of-a-kind
gadgets with no purpose.
Could he fix anything, everything?
I don't know, but
he could improvise like
Coltrane.

As he got old he got supple like
old leather, overgrown like an old
garden, it was all good.
Except, of course, that his machine,
like all machines, began to
wear out. There are only so many parts
that can be replaced. And I think he
was interested in the feel of each
day, rather than saving up
as many as he could.
And I missed my chance.
I missed my chance and I've
almost forgiven myself for it.
I missed my chance to learn
what this spirited man thought
about the death that was
closing in on him as surely as nightfall, I
missed my chance to talk about fear, or grace, or
choices, I missed my chance to
be a man with him, to face down a
mystery. Instead, I let my
mother's worry rub off, I suggested that he
might want to slow down, eat better.
Christ Almighty.

If I were a younger man I would
be disgusted with myself, but I'm not
a younger man, and thank God I
know that Pop loved me and let it
slide.
Still.
Were you scared Pop?
What was it like?

Now the mysterious cluttered workbench
is mine. I alone know the blueprints for
the half-built gimcracks, the unfinished
gizmos.
I don't want to live forever
either. I'd rather go
tomorrow, happy, busy, than
to be a 100 year-old
Styrofoam likeness of a
man.
Not that anyone is
asking, but I'm not scared.
And if it is today?
So far, it's just like
any other
day.

Bottom-of-my-heart thanks go to:

Elizabeth Garber, Sharon Mesmer, Jenni Lyn Cooper, Rick, Chris, Matt, Sonny and Jack; Tony Forte, Perry King, Kent from Tex-i-co, Hal Owen, Kathy Polenberg, Joe-babe, Linda V, Adam W, Jim & Sondra Zoot, Jett, Giff, Karen Jalenfy, Ken Gross, Cathy Melio, Al & Lorna Crichton, Wes McNair, Betsy Sholl, Matt DiGangi, Laura Hird, Trace & Martin, Ellen Parker, PH Madore, Denise Dee, Laura V, Amy Silver, Bro Tim, Bill Seldon, Joan Duckett, David Hadju, Jo Ann Beard, Andy Stone, Old friends at the HRC in NYC, Kenny at the Bitter End; the Trademarks, True Blue, the Juke Savages, my midcoast poetry friends, my family, everyone.
And, of course, Susan.
Thank you.

Did I mention Wally Kulakowski?

(SWEET)

New and selected poems
(2006)

A hardy weed in the garden of American poetry, Dave Morrison's work is equal parts blue collar skepticism, jazzy dreamscapes, and dark humor.

"A tidal wave of outrageous creativity; a wild rift of lines that leave you out of breath, fascinated, manipulated, articulated. Watch out!"
- Elizabeth Garber, author of *Pierced by the Seasons* and *Listening Inside the Dance* -

"So there's obviously no f**king with Dave Morrison's writing...read [it] by candlelight while drinking straight from the bottle, the radio playing softly in the corner."
– Matt DiGangi editor *Thieves Jargon* -

"...like Mary Oliver with a leather jacket and a sense of humor."
-Sharon Mesmer author of *HALF ANGEL, HALF LUNCH* and *THE EMPTY QUARTER* –

Available at better bookstores, lulu.com, amazon.com, and B&N.com

About the Author
This is the author's second book of poetry, not counting the 20-odd journals in the box in the basement. DM was born 7/24/1959 in Reading, a suburb of Boston and home of the Rockets. School? Next. Discovered guitar at 16, playing bars at 17, two kickass Boston bands that came this close (the Trademarks and True Blue). Then, the best gift: Susan. Married, moved to NYC. Waiting table, solo gigs in Village bars, saved by the mighty Juke Savages, who were never meant for small stages and 'showcase' gigs. 40 year-old freshman in the New School Writing Program. Goodbye band life. Hello Maine.

And you're a Prima ballerina
on a spring afternoon –
Change on into the Wolfman
howling at the moon

Awoooooooooh!

New York Dolls

www.ingramcontent.com/pod-product-compliance
Lightning Source LLC
Chambersburg PA
CBHW021020090426
42738CB00007B/846